MY FIRST DAY

TRANSITIONING FROM GIRLHOOD TO WOMANHOOD

SECOND EDITION

BY YASMINE BEN SALMI

 | MY FIRST DAY
TRANSITIONING FROM GIRLHOOD TO WOMANHOOD

Published by The Choice Is Yours Publishing

Copyright © Yasmine Ben Salmi

The author asserts the moral right under the Copyright, Designs and Patents Act 1988 to be identified as the author of this work.

All Rights reserved. No part of this publication may be reproduced, stored in a retrieval system or transmitted, in any form or by any means without the prior consent of the author, nor be otherwise circulated in any form of binding or cover other than that which it is published and without a similar condition being imposed on the subsequent purchaser.

Copyright © 2022 Yasmine Ben Salmi
All rights reserved.

HARDBACK *ISBN:* 978-1-913310-90-5
PAPERBACK *ISBN:* 978-1-913310-93-6

MY FIRST DAY

TRANSITIONING FROM GIRLHOOD TO WOMANHOOD

BY YASMINE BEN SALMI

DEDICATIONS

DEDICATIONS

This book is dedicated to young girls who are going to start their menstrual cycle and some tips and tricks on how you can have a smooth first day.

I also want to dedicate this book to my parents, Sabrina and Mohamed Ben Salmi.
My brothers and sister: Lashai Ben Salmi
, aka Dreampreneur, Tray-Sean Ben Salmi
aka T7 & Child Genius Advisor, Paolo
Ben Salmi, aka Pint Size Adventurer, Amire Ben
Salmi, aka Mr Intelligent. My nan Mary Paul
Founder of Mary Paul's Creations. Rev Dr Trevor Adams, Apostle Linda Edwards, Abuelo & Abuela Alan & Justine Shelton.

And to you for choosing this book; I hope you learn a lot.

Let's embark on this journey together.

ACKNOWLEDGEMENTS

ACKNOWLEDGEMENTS

I want to thank all my family and friends for their love, support and encouragement because I genuinely appreciate having each and every one of them in my life.

I want to take this opportunity to write a special message from my heart to yours. Please do not be afraid when it comes to the sacred time of starting your period because it is a part of becoming a woman. Surrender to the process because your body knows exactly what to do during your transition from girlhood to womanhood. I hope that from this book, you will learn some new things about your period that you have never known before; remember to trust the process and use the tips that I am giving you in this book, and most importantly, have fun learning new things about your body.

I believe in you – you've got this! Take a deep breath and trust the process because everything will be okay.

Just know that you are not alone because I am right here with you, embarking on this sacred journey together with every young lady who is also transitioning.

TABLE OF CONTENTS

- Introduction **9**
- What Is A Period? **12**
- When do Most Girls Get Their First Periods? **17**
- What Causes A Period? **22**
- How Does Ovulation Relate To Periods? **27**
- Will I Have Periods Regularly When My Menstruation Begins? **32**
- Should I Use A Pad, Tampon or Menstrual Cup? **37**
- How Much Blood Comes Out? **43**
- Will I Have Periods For The Rest Of My Life? **48**
- What Is PMS? **53**
- What Can I Do About Period Cramps? **58**
- Why Do We Call It Menstruation? **63**
- Your Amazing Body **68**
- Should I Watch Out For Any Problems **78**
- Periods are Natural **83**
- My First Day Letter **88**
- Discharge **95**
- Surprise Bonus Chapter: I AM Jewel Pad - Reign **103**
- Track Your Period **131**
- Surprise Bonus Chapter: Q & A **138**
- Bonus Chapter From Her-Rah! 1st Bra **145**
- My First Day Journal **154**
- About The Author **177**

INTRODUCTION

INTRODUCTION

I wrote this book to help girls learn more about the transition from girlhood to womanhood.

I realised it is taboo to even mention a girl's menstrual cycle in some countries, and I want to change that by writing this book. In this book, you will find chapters that will help to answer your burning questions and an excellent period tracker at the end; you will also get a few bonus chapters and some more knowledge about your amazing female body, so you can learn more about your menstrual cycle and some changes you might go through, and how to deal with them.

In my secondary school, many girls started their periods without knowing what was happening to their bodies. I remember a girl saying she drank cranberry juice, and it came out again later. Another girl started her cycle in class, finding a blood stain on her seat and uniform. I genuinely believe that my book could help girls learn about what is happening to their bodies and reassure them that it is all part of the natural process of becoming a woman. I dream of empowering girls, so they do not have to be taken by surprise on their first day. In my family, my mother, sister and grandmother talked to me to prepare me for my first day, and I pray that my book will help you to understand more about your amazing female body.

Remember to love your body no matter what; when you choose to do that, you will trust your body with what has to come and know that it isn't that scary!

So, I hope you enjoy reading this book.

WHAT IS A PERIOD?

WHAT IS A PERIOD?

A period is the part of the menstrual cycle that most girls start when they're about 12. Still, they can begin as early as 8, so it's important to talk to girls from an early age to ensure that they're prepared before the big day, as I like to call it, transitioning from girlhood into womanhood.

Many parents feel awkward talking about periods and their experience, especially with pre-teen girls, who can easily get embarrassed.

Please check out this video by Dr Simi, who talks about periods and how to care for the female body.

YouTube:
https://www.youtube.com/watch?v=ajM1xtS9Kp8

"When you choose to accept who you are, you will have no space for those who disagree."

- Self-acceptance is the key to your emotional development. List 3-5 things that you can do to implement more self-acceptance into your life.
- Create a period playlist that you can listen to each month to help you feel better.
- Invigorate your mind and body with a cold shower and feel the benefits of cold water therapy.

_____
_____
_____
_____
_____
_____
_____
_____
_____
_____
_____
_____
_____
_____ MY FIRST DAY

NOTES
MY FIRST DAY

————————————— MY FIRST DAY

WHEN DO MOST GIRLS GET THEIR FIRST PERIOD?

WHEN DO MOST GIRLS GET THEIR FIRST PERIOD?

Most girls get their period when they are about 12 years of age. But it has been known that you can start your period between the ages of 8,10, and 15 years old. And that is fine, as every girl's body has its schedule that it runs on. There is no specific age for a girl to start her period, but there are some clues that it will begin soon:

The first sign is when you have Vaginal discharge fluid (like a mucus texture) that you might see or feel on your underwear. This discharge usually begins around six months to a year before you start your first period.

Most of the time, girls usually start their periods around two years after their breasts begin to develop.

Right after your breast starts to form, you'll start growing pubic hair down there, it will be soft and thin at first, but it'll get harsh in texture over time, and after that, just around one to two years, your period is likely to arrive.

One thing to know is that your body is just transitioning, so don't be scared and remember to love yourself no matter what.

"Learn to love yourself unconditionally."

- Unconditional love is a good starting point. List 3-5 ways you can begin to love yourself unconditionally.
- Explore a food market.
- Learn a new dance routine, and if it feels right, why don't you film it and share it on TikTok? I hear all the cool kids are doing it!

MY FIRST DAY

NOTES
MY FIRST DAY

_____
_____
_____
_____
_____
_____
_____
_____
_____
_____
_____
_____ MY FIRST DAY

WHAT CAUSES A PERIOD?

WHAT CAUSES A PERIOD?

A period occurs because of changes in hormones in the female body. Hormones are chemical messengers that are active throughout the body.

The ovaries release the female hormones called (estrogen and progesterone). These hormones cause the lining of the uterus to build up.

The Built-up lining is then ready for a fertilized egg to attach to and develop. If there is no fertilized egg, the lining then breaks down and bleeds, this occurs over and over again each month causing what we know as a period; our bodies are so magnificent, right?

The lining usually takes a month to build and break down. That is why most girls and women receive their periods around once a month.

"You are beautiful and
perfect just the way you are."

- You are **BEAUTIFUL**, **PERFECT** and **UNIQUE** just the way you are. No one can dance your dance, no one can sing your song, and no one can talk your talk. **JUST BE YOU** because everyone else is already taken. List 3-5 things you like about yourself and 3-5 things other people like about you.
- Treat yourself to a spa day and indulge in a pre-menstrual massage, pedicure and facial in the comfort of your home.
- Are you struggling to sleep? Get up early and watch the sunrise and visualise your deepest desires.

_____
_____
_____
_____
_____
_____
_____
_____
_____
_____
_____
_____
_____
_____ MY FIRST DAY

NOTES
MY FIRST DAY

_____

_____ MY FIRST DAY

HOW DOES OVULATION RELATE TO PERIODS?

HOW DOES OVULATION RELATE TO PERIODS?

Ovulation is the release of an egg from the ovaries. The hormones that cause the uterus lining to build up also cause an egg to leave one of the ovaries. The egg then travels through a very thin tube called the (fallopian tube) to make its way to the uterus.

If the egg is then fertilized by a sperm cell, it attaches to the uterus wall, where it develops into a baby over time. If the egg is not fertilized, the uterus lining breaks down and bleeds, causing what we know as a period.

"Be less afraid of changing old habits and more open to creating new ones."

- Learning healthy new habits is the difference that can make a huge difference in your life. List 3-5 new routines that you will implement in your life.
- Visit an independent bookstore or library and stock up on books to read during your period.
- Put together a period package that includes your favourite treats and self-care essentials and post it to yourself so it arrives just in time for your period.

MY FIRST DAY

NOTES
MY FIRST DAY

_____
_____
_____
_____
_____
_____
_____
_____
_____
_____
_____
_____ MY FIRST DAY

> WILL I HAVE PERIODS REGULARLY WHEN MY MENSTRUATION BEGINS?

WILL I HAVE PERIODS REGULARLY WHEN MY MENSTRUATION BEGINS?

The menstrual cycle is the monthly hormonal cycle the female body goes through to prepare for pregnancy. Your menstrual cycle is calculated from the first day of your period up to the first day of your next period.

For the first few years after a girl starts her period, it may not come regularly, and this is normal at first. Within 2-3 years after a girl's first period, it should be coming around every 4-5 weeks; some girls usually start their periods every six weeks.

Periods usually happen every 4-5 weeks, but some girls can receive their period a little later or more often than usual.

"Surrender to the process of transitioning from girlhood to womanhood."

- Surrendering to transitioning from girlhood to womanhood will help you create more ease and flow in your life. List 3-5 ways to learn how to go with the flow more often.
- Build a gentle skincare routine or a homemade face mask with calming and anti-inflammatory ingredients.
- Have a long, hot bubble bath with essential oils, mellow music, and a good book.

MY FIRST DAY

NOTES
MY FIRST DAY

———————————————————————
———————————————————————
———————————————————————
———————————————————————
———————————————————————
———————————————————————
———————————————————————
———————————————————————
———————————————————————
———————————————————————
——————————— MY FIRST DAY

SHOULD I USE A PAD, TAMPON, OR MENSTRUAL CUP?

SHOULD I USE A PAD, TAMPON, OR MENSTRUAL CUP?

You have many choices about how to deal with period blood. You may need to find which way works better for you. Some girls prefer using only one method, and others switch between different forms, depending on which one seems more comfortable.

- Most girls use pads when they first get their period. Pads are made of cotton and come in lots of sizes and shapes. They have sticky strips underneath the pad to attach to your underwear; you should not leave a pad on for more than 3-4 hours.

- Many girls find tampons more convenient than pads, especially when playing sports or swimming. A tampon is a cotton plug placed inside a girl's vagina. Most tampons come with an applicator that guides the tampon into place. The tampon absorbs the blood from your period. You should not leave a tampon in for more than 8 hours because this can increase your risk of a severe infection called (toxic shock syndrome or TSS for short).

- Some girls prefer a menstrual cup. Most menstrual cups are made of silicone material. To use a menstrual cup, a girl must insert it into her vagina. Once it is in place, it holds the blood until the girl empties it.

- Most girls need to change their pads, tampons, or menstrual cups about 3-6 times a day.

- I use pads as I find them more convenient to use. My mum and big sister also find it more comfortable, but as you start your period, you will find methods that make you comfortable.

"Getting to know yourself a little more every day is a good starting place."

- Getting to know yourself a little more daily is a good starting place. List 3-5 things you learned about yourself and your body today.
- Cook a nourishing meal with a loved one and indulge.
- Head to the park with a loved one and lay down on a blanket as you watch the clouds and world go by. See what you can spot in the sky?

_____
_____
_____
_____
_____
_____
_____
_____
_____
_____
_____
_____
_____
_____
_____ MY FIRST DAY

NOTES
MY FIRST DAY

_____
_____
_____
_____
_____
_____
_____
_____
_____
_____
_____
_____ MY FIRST DAY

HOW MUCH BLOOD COMES OUT?

HOW MUCH BLOOD COMES OUT?

It may look like a lot of blood, but throughout your whole menstrual cycle, you lose less than 16 tablespoons; when I first heard that, I was thinking, are you sure, because I think I saw a lot more than that.

Most women will lose less than 16 teaspoons of blood; in millilitres, it is around 80mls if their period is heavy. However, the average tends to be about 6 to 8 teaspoons.

You may wonder why a lot of blood comes out when you have your period.

So, it's perfectly normal if you see any clumps from time to time during your period. These are blood clots that may contain tissue. As the uterus sheds its lining, the tissue leaves the body looking like a natural part of the menstrual cycle. So, when you see blood clots, they are usually nothing to be concerned about; but if you do have any concerns, you might want to seek medical attention.

"I am working towards becoming the best version of me."

- Take a deep breath and know that you are working towards becoming the best version of yourself. Remember to be kind to yourself daily and take one step at a time.
- Plan a mini-break or a day trip to visit with a loved one when your period is over. Choose somewhere you've never been before, it will give you something to look forward to.
- Chat with a good friend on the phone and reminisce for hours.

———————————————— MY FIRST DAY

NOTES
MY FIRST DAY

--- MY FIRST DAY

WILL I HAVE PERIODS FOR THE REST OF MY LIFE?

WILL I HAVE PERIODS FOR THE REST OF MY LIFE?

The answer to this question is no; you will not have your period for the rest of your life because when women reach menopause around the age of 45-55, their periods will permanently stop.

Also, another factor is that when women are pregnant, they will also not have a period until their baby is delivered. So, you won't have to worry about having a period for the rest of your life.

Let's quickly talk about menopause; let's start with the first question what happens during menopause?

Well, we already know menopause happens when we reach the age of 45-55, but what happens to our bodies?

When we are going through menopause, 2 of the most common signs include:

1: Irregular periods
2: Hot flashes throughout the body

"Self-care is not selfish; it is absolutely paramount."

- Self-care is not selfish; it is absolutely paramount. List 3-5 things you can do to take care of yourself.
- Take time to slow down, rest and reflect truly.
- Get lost in period content on Youtube and learn about other people's flows and first-time stories.

MY FIRST DAY

NOTES
MY FIRST DAY

_____
_____
_____
_____
_____
_____
_____
_____
_____
_____
_____
_____ MY FIRST DAY

WHAT IS PMS?

WHAT IS PMS?

PMS is the abbreviation for (premenstrual syndrome) it is when a girl has emotional and physical symptoms that can happen before or even during her period. These symptoms can include moodiness, sadness, anxiety, bloating, and acne. The symptoms disappear after the first few days of being on your period.

Here is a tip that can help to treat your PMS symptoms:

Control your diet; what I mean by this is to control your eating, so while on your period, try to avoid foods that may contain:

- Salt
- Caffeine
- Sugar
- Fizzy

Some other ways to reduce PMS is by performing light stretches, as stretches are known to help with period pains and menstrual cramps.

And also, a significant factor to consider is reducing your stress levels by taking time to relax and recharge, perhaps journal, watch one of your favourite shows, or spend time with yourself. Listening to music is my favourite, especially when I have a playlist of my favourite songs.

"Either you love yourself first, or you wait for society to accept you; either way, 'The Choice Is Yours."

- Either love yourself first or wait for society to accept you; either way, 'The Choice Is Yours'. List 3-5 ways that you can do to love yourself.
- Treat yourself to an item on your wish list
- Get creative on Canva, Adobe or paper

_____
_____
_____
_____
_____
_____
_____
_____
_____
_____
_____
_____
_____
_____
_____ MY FIRST DAY

NOTES
MY FIRST DAY

_____
_____
_____
_____
_____
_____
_____
_____
_____
_____
_____
_____ MY FIRST DAY

WHAT CAN I DO ABOUT PERIOD CRAMPS?

WHAT CAN I DO ABOUT PERIOD CRAMPS?

Many girls have cramps during their period, especially during the first few days. If you are experiencing any cramps and they are bothering you, you can try the following:

A warm heating pad/hot water bottle on your stomach is a female family favourite, the synonyms, but my mother and sister love to use this, as it calms down the pain and soothes it.

You could try taking ibuprofen, which is a form of pain relief, but please ask your parents/guardians for advice if you are underage or seek medical attention.

Near the end of the book, you will find a chapter called your amazing body, where you will find some more tips on dealing with cramps and all those feelings we might experience that aren't exceptionally comfortable.

"What makes you happy?
How can you experience
more of that?"

- What makes you happy? List 3-5 things that make you happy. How can you experience more of that?
- Fill up a hot water bottle and rest it on your belly while you lie on the couch or in bed watching inspiring TED Talks, a movie or whatever brings you joy.
- Unplug for the day! Sometimes the best cure for challenging period pains is limiting the amount of social media you consume.

_____
_____
_____
_____
_____
_____
_____
_____
_____
_____
_____
_____ MY FIRST DAY

NOTES
MY FIRST DAY

--- MY FIRST DAY

WHY DO WE CALL IT MENSTRUATION?

WHY DO WE CALL IT MENSTRUATION?

First of all, why do we call it a "menstrual cycle" anyway?

Well, it turns out it comes from the Latin word "menses", meaning the word "month", so when we think of the word menstrual, keep the word menses in mind.

It makes sense providing the fact that women receive their periods once a month.

Oh, another word is period which is rooted from the Greek word "peri" and "hodos" and all together "perihodos", which means "around" and "way or path". This eventually turned into the Latin word "periodus" meaning "recurring cycle", when translated into the English term "period" to describe menstruation which began in the early 1800s so when you put it all together, it all adds up to the words that we now know today.

Wow, we learned a lot about history and etymology (the study of words and their origins).

"Knowing your worth is more important than others not recognizing it."

- Knowing your worth is more important than others not recognizing it. List 3-5 things that you know you deserve eg I am worthy to receive love, kindness and respect, I am worthy.
- Don't let your hormones get the better of you. Practice positive self-talk to boost your mood and love for yourself.
- Changed out of your PJs, open up your wardrobe, choose a fancy but comfy outfit, and do your hair. I guarantee you'll feel more uplifted in no time.
- Listen to an audiobook and get lost in your imagination.

_____
_____
_____
_____
_____
_____
_____
_____
_____
_____
_____
_____
_____ MY FIRST DAY

NOTES
MY FIRST DAY

_____
_____
_____
_____
_____
_____
_____
_____
_____
_____
_____
_____ MY FIRST DAY

YOUR AMAZING BODY

YOUR AMAZING BODY

As you transition from girlhood to womanhood, always remember to love yourself and trust the process. If you feel uncomfortable or unsure, feel free to speak to your parents/guardians and seek medical attention. Just know that your body is amazing and knows exactly what to do to take good care of yourself during your menstrual cycle. I want you to know that you have an amazing body and your body already knows exactly what to do, so please learn to trust your body.

SELF CARE

Many girls have cramps while on their period, especially in the first few days. If you are experiencing any cramps, take good care of yourself.

BATH SALTS

Well, this is one of my favourites because I absolutely love bath salts; the ones I love to use the most are bath salts with real roses in them because they smell soooo goooood.

HOT WATER BOTTLE

A hot water bottle can reduce cramps, and it can also help to relax you. In fact, my big sister Lashai Ben Salmi and my mum Sabrina Ben Salmi find it really helpful to use a hot water bottle while they are on their periods, so hopefully, it can help you.

ESSENTIAL OILS

Okay, we are now getting into this, essential oils, essential oils, essential oils… one more time, essential oils. I imagine that you get the impression that I lovvvvve essential oils. It is said that using essential oils such as Lavender, Clove, Cinnamon, and Rose as these essential oils are typically applied to the abdomen for seven days before menstruation as they are believed to reduce the amount of pain experienced and even the amount of blood you will lose can also be reduced. It can make you smell so nice too.

HERBAL TEA

Drinking herbal tea can often help with menstrual cramps: Hibiscus, Chamomile, Rose Petals, Raspberry Leaf Tea, and one of my favourite teas to drink while on my period is Lemon and Ginger tea. Each tea will affect everyone differently, so be sure to try a few and choose which ones you like most.

BATH BOMBS

A bath bomb adds emollients and softeners to your bath's water that moisturizes your skin. No matter what your skin type, the beneficial ingredients in bath bombs have a soothing effect on the body and uhhhhh It's so lovely.

JOURNAL

Recording details like the strength of your flow, the severity of cramps or any symptoms you may have because it could really help you make sense of what a typical period looks like.

PADS/CUPS/TAMPONS

There are many different options, but in my opinion, pads are the best, but you can choose which works best for you; one of the things I would recommend when buying pads is always to get the organic ones.

BRUSH TEETH

Well, you may not have known this, but our periods tremendously affect our teeth, well not in the way that you think, but research shows that hormonal highs and lows can impact your oral health. The symptoms you may experience during your period may be a sense of soreness in your mouth, with your gums swelling and becoming more prone to bleeding, so one thing I'm going to end on is… "Brush Your Teeth".

BRUSH YOUR HAIR

Well, I know this might sound like a ridiculous thing to do but trust me, you will thank me later. Your skin and scalp change in response to hormonal variations occurring throughout your period. Some people report more bad hair days around their period; many of the changes you may associate with your hair throughout your cycle are due to the changes in oil production from your hormones.

EMOTIONS

It is always important to acknowledge and express your emotions. Sometimes your hormones may cause you to feel slightly out of character, and during these times, it's important to honour your feelings and communicate how you feel with loved ones. You might be wondering what causes your emotions to get all over the place; it has a lot to do with when your estrogen level decreases during the surge and the progesterone level start to increase. During the luteal phase, luteinizing hormone and follicle-stimulating hormone levels decrease. The ruptured follicle then closes after it releases the egg, forming a corpus leteum that produces progesterone.

SLEEP

Some girls may experience some cramps, and this may interrupt your sleep. So please do some research about sleep hacks to help you drift off and maintain a peaceful sleep throughout the night. Sleeping well at night will give your body time to rest and repair during this sacred process.

LIGHT EXERCISE

Light exercise can often help some girls improve their mood and increase circulation.

FRIENDSHIPS

Having a healthy relationship with a close friend is good for your health, so it can have a substantial positive impact on you while you are on your period too. So be sure to spend quality time with a close friend when you need emotional support.

"Never regret anything you said or did when it came from a place of love."

- Never regret anything you said or did when it came from a place of love. List 3-5 things you have said or done from a position of love.
- Get out in nature and maybe even walk barefoot if you feel comfortable. A combination of movement and fresh air can make a huge difference.
- Do a high-intensity workout to get your endorphins flowing through your body. Do some research to find period-friendly workouts.

MY FIRST DAY

NOTES
MY FIRST DAY

MY FIRST DAY

SHOULD I WATCH OUT FOR ANY PROBLEMS?

SHOULD I WATCH OUT FOR ANY PROBLEMS?

Most girls don't have any problems with their periods: But call your doctor if you:

- Are 15 years old and haven't started your period

- Have your period for more than two years, and it still doesn't come regularly (about every 4-5 weeks)

- Have bleeding between periods

- Have severe cramps that don't get better with ibuprofen or naproxen.

- Have very heavy bleeding that goes through a pad or tampon faster than every 1 hour.

- Have periods that last more than about a week

- Have severe PMS that gets in the way of your everyday activities.

Always trust your intuition, so if for any reason you feel the need to speak to your parents or seek medical attention, please do not hesitate to do so.

"Loving your body is the best thing that you can do."

- Loving your body is the best thing that you can do. List 3-5 ways you can take better care of your body.
- Head to the cinema with a loved one.
- Get dressed up and head out somewhere with a loved one.

_____
_____
_____
_____
_____
_____
_____
_____
_____
_____
_____
_____
_____
_____
_____
_____
_____
_____
_____ MY FIRST DAY

NOTES
MY FIRST DAY

_____

_____

_____

_____

_____

_____

_____

_____

_____

_____

_____

_____

_____ MY FIRST DAY

PERIODS ARE NATURAL

PERIODS ARE NATURAL

Periods are a natural, healthy part of a girl's life. They shouldn't get in the way of exercising, having fun, and enjoying life. If you have questions about periods, ask your doctor, a parent, a health teacher, a school nurse, or an older sister.

I think that it is important to have someone to talk to, especially a female; I really find that when I talk to my mother and sister about having my period, we can then agree on the things that may have happened to them and they can give me advise on what to do.

So, if you haven't got a sister, ask a medical teacher at your school, your mother, or just female relatives.

So, you're not alone!

Also, we've got the internet; go ahead and start filling up all your tabs on google or safari about tips and tricks; you'll have so much knowledge that when you have kids, they won't even need the internet. Well, that's if you don't forget, simply trust the process.

"Be sure to speak uplifting words to yourself because all the cells in your body are listening."

- Be sure to speak uplifting words to yourself because all the cells in your body are listening. List 3-5 positive affirmations.
- Wash your bed sheets, pyjamas, towels and underwear. Freshly cleaned bedding and clothes will help to leave your mood.
- Tidy and declutter your personal spaces. It will help to make your environment feel so much better as you clear out the old in order to make space to welcome the new.

MY FIRST DAY

NOTES
MY FIRST DAY

_____
_____
_____
_____
_____
_____
_____
_____
_____
_____
_____
_____
_____ MY FIRST DAY

MY FIRST DAY LETTER

MY FIRST DAY LETTER

This part of the book is specifically for your parents or guardians to complete. In the following pages, they will be able to write you a special letter that you can read on the first day of your period to help lift your mood and make you feel loved and supported. The purpose of this letter is to encourage you on your first day should it happen while you are apart from loved ones.

Dear Mum/Dad//Aunt/Uncle/Cousin/Grandpa/Grandma/Guardian, start this letter by inserting their name into the allocated space in the letter template. Go ahead and write a special note with love to lift their mood on the first day of their period.

I think that writing a letter to your daughter/niece/cousin/granddaughter etc., for their first day is the difference that will make the difference for their first day. This will help them feel loved and supported when they know someone they love wrote them a special letter for the first day.

Dear_____

_____
_____
_____
_____
_____
_____
_____
_____
_____
_____
_____
_____
_____
_____
_____
_____
_____
_____
_____

From:_____
_____ MY FIRST DAY

Dear_____

_____
_____
_____
_____
_____
_____
_____
_____
_____
_____
_____
_____
_____
_____
_____
_____
_____

From:_____
_____MY FIRST DAY

"Love your body no matter what."

- Love your body no matter what. List 3-5 ways you can love your body no matter what.
- Hit the reset button and get organised in life. Take a couple of days to get back on track and nurture your creative flow.

MY FIRST DAY

NOTES
MY FIRST DAY

_____
_____
_____
_____
_____
_____
_____
_____
_____
_____
_____
_____ MY FIRST DAY

DISCHARGE

DISCHARGE

It is important to keep an eye on the different colours of your discharge pre-period, during your period and after your period.

White – Thick, white discharge is common at the beginning and end of your cycle as long as the normal white discharge is not accompanied by itching. But if this is the case, this discharge may be indicating a yeast infection.

Clear and watery – This is "fertile" mucous and means you are ovulating.

Clear and stretchy – This occurs at different times of your cycle and can be particularly heavy after exercise.

Yellow and green – This may indicate an infection, especially if it's thick or clumpy like cottage cheese or has a foul odour.

Brown – This may happen right after your period as your body is "cleaning out" your vagina. Old blood looks brown.

Spotting/ blood spotting – This may occur mid-cycle or when ovulating. Sometimes early in pregnancy, you may have spotting or a brownish discharge at the time your period would normally come.

If you have any concerns, please do not hesitate to speak to your parents and seek medical attention.

Do some research.

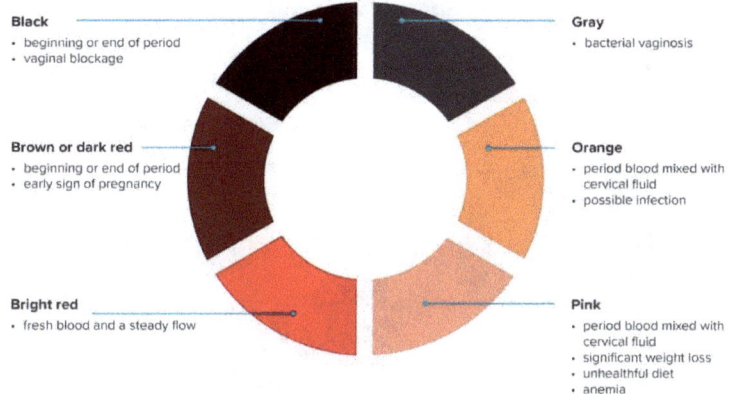

Do some research.

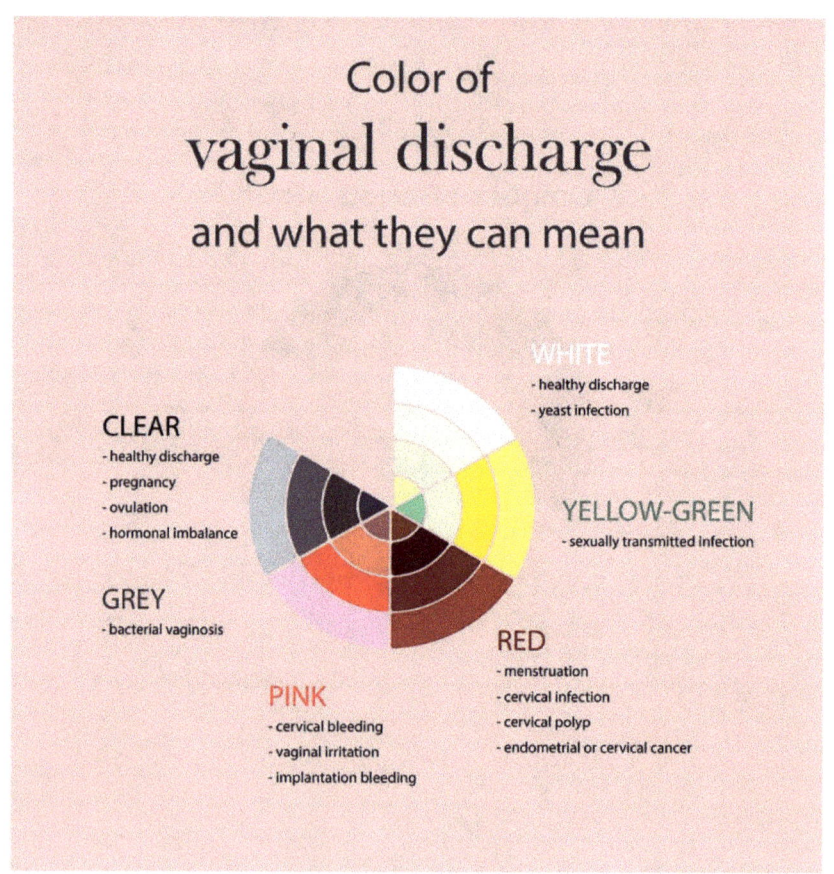

Do some research.

"Give yourself permission to take time out."

- Give yourself permission to take time out. List 3-5 ways you can take time out to relax and recharge.
- Write 10 things that you are grateful for
- List 10 affirmations

MY FIRST DAY

NOTES
MY FIRST DAY

_____
_____
_____
_____
_____
_____
_____
_____
_____
_____
_____
_____— MY FIRST DAY

SURPRISE BONUS CHAPTER: I AM JEWEL PADS - REIGN

SURPRISE BONUS CHAPTER:
I AM JEWEL PADS - REIGN

SURPRISE BONUS CHAPTER: I AM JEWEL PADS - REIGN

You are welcome to use this or ANYTHING from our site WWW.IAM.JEWELPADS.COM

I have not brought Qiana into the picture since our initial conversation.
I really think it's best to talk in detail about our products from a place of experience...
Your thoughts...?

Discover The Value We Provide
Jewel is passionate about redefining your life with our revolutionary and life-changing products.

Reign Sanitary Napkins

All around the world, women are excited to experience Reign Sanitary Napkins. Reign pads are infused with Nobel Prize Winning material "Graphene". The Graphene infused strip may provide various health benefits that may improve micro-circulation, may promote cell activity and may also help support a healthy metabolism. In addition, it may help inhibit harmful bacteria growth, allowing females to feel comfortable and, most of all dry. Reign has five variations to meet your flow: Ultra-Thin Panty Liner for everyday use, Very Light Panty Liner with wings and light absorbency, Moderate, Heavy, and Super Heavy Overnight Flow.

8 LAYERS OF PROTECTION
10X MORE ABSORBENT

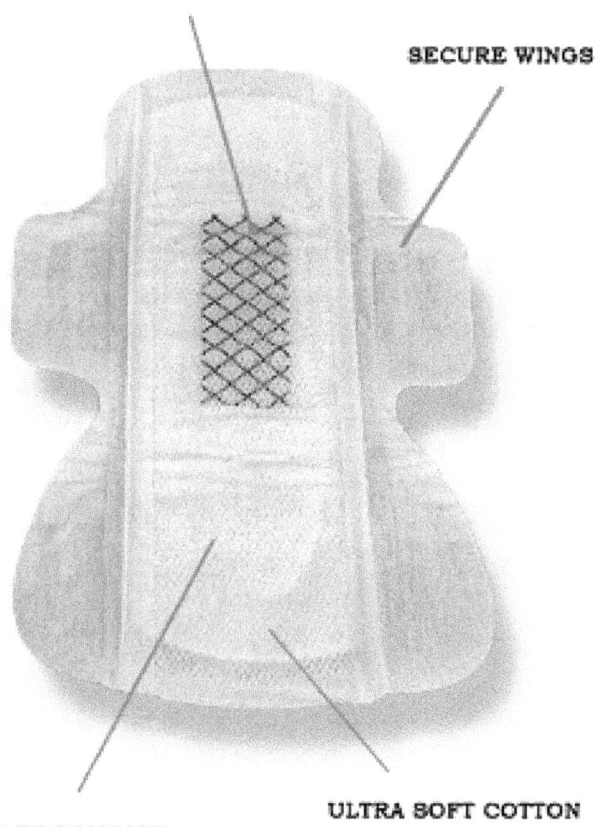

GRAPHENE MATERIAL

SECURE WINGS

SAFE POLYMER

ULTRA SOFT COTTON

Jewel has an Innovative design that is made with a strip infused with Nobel Prize winning material "Graphene".
The infused Graphene strip may provide various health benefits that potentially:

- Help relieve painful abdominal cramps
- Help balance the body's PH
- Help Eliminate harmful bacteria
- Help with aroma
- Help fight fatigue
- Boost metabolism
- Boost Immune system
- Graphene moves heat away from your core and contains vibrational energy

JEWEL PREMIUM SANITARY NAPKINS

HTTP://ROCHELLESWEALTH.COM

Our goal at Jewel is to help you look as good as you feel. Our mission is to develop products and opportunities that give you the power to project the confidence that radiates from within. Whatever your age, background or lifestyle, Jewel provides you with products that will improve your life and your lifestyle. We invest our research and development into creating products that not only offer exceptional results, but are also multi-functional, addressing many different aspects that affect your life.

Layer 1 – Reign Sanitary Napkins has a 3-dimensional layer, and leak guard sides for extra protection against leakage.

Layer 2 – The 2nd layer of Reign has a ultra-soft cotton top layer, extremely comfortable an soft to the skin.

Layer 3 – The 3rd layer of Reign is an Innovative design that offers a Nobel Prize Winning material "Graphene" infused strip. The infused Graphene strip may provide various health benefits to potentially help with circulatory health, cell activity, and metabolic health. In addition, it may help inhibit harmful bacteria growth.

Layer 4 – The 4th layer of Reign offers an Air-laid design for extra protection against undesired leakage. Our innovative design is adept at moving the moisture away from the body, so you feel comfortable and dry.

Layer 5 – The 5th layer of Reign is designed with a safe, super absorbent polymer, absorbing up to 10x more menstrual flow than traditional sanitary napkins.

Layer 6 – The 6th layer of Reign offers reinforcement against moisture. We have added an additional layer of Air-laid. Reign Sanitary Napkins Innovative design is adept at moving the moisture away from the body, not only do you feel comfortable and dry we have gone step further to add extra protection against leakage.

Layer 7 – The 7th layer of Reign offers extreme breathability, which eliminates heat and undesirable moisture. The micro-perforated bottom layer offers air dispersion to keep the area cool and most of all dry. This may help prevent the growth of harmful bacteria and odor.

Layer 8 – The 8th layer of Reign offers a durable, agricultural-grade adhesive, without the use of toxic chemicals. Many manufacturers use a construction-grade adhesive, which can be extremely detrimental to a female's most precious area, as well as the planet.
Reign Sanitary Napkins are individually wrapped and sealed with a single-strip tape closure design to keep the product secure and protected from any outside elements.

Jewel Mission Statement
Protect The Most Precious Jewel In The World, YOU!

Our mission is to raise awareness by informing both teens and women globally who suffer in silence with pain, heavy bleeding, unhealthy menstrual cycles and the potential toxicity of tampon use.

Our goal is to bring light to a taboo subject of female cycles, that has silenced females from all cultures for many years.

Our platform will educate females on the important roles of keeping a healthy cycle by encouraging getting active, healthy eating, healthy product choices and community awareness events.

The silent suffering stops with the voice of our campaign.

Reign Fundraiser

Help Your Organization Reach Their Financial Goals!

Help your organization support the Reign Premium Sanitary Napkin Fundraiser. Your organization has collaborated with the Justice For My Jewel Campaign (jfmj.org), which sheds light on the silent suffering females have endured because of the chemical and inferior makeup of the tampons and sanitary napkins made available to them. The campaign has become the voice of the silent suffering and Reign has become the healthier alternative.

Benefits of Supporting Your Organization

Helps support the organizations mission
Helps raise community awareness
Helps them reach their financial goals
Helps protect women and young girls

Reign Pads are infused with Nobel Prize Winning material "Graphene". The infused Graphene strip may provide various health benefits that potentially:

- Help relieve painful abdominal cramps
- Help balance the body's PH
- Help Eliminate harmful bacteria
- Help with aroma
- Help fight fatigue
- Boost metabolism
- Boost Immune system
- Graphene moves heat away from your core and contains vibrational energy
- Benefits of Graphene Material

Reign Pads are infused with Nobel Prize Winning material "Graphene".

The infused Graphene strip may provide various health benefits that potentially:

- Help relieve painful abdominal cramps
- Help balance the body's PH
- Help Eliminate harmful bacteria
- Help with aroma
- Help fight fatigue
- Boost metabolism
- Boost Immune system
- Graphene moves heat away from your core and contains vibrational energy

- **Layer 1** – Reign Sanitary Napkins has a 3-dimensional layer, and leak guard sides for extra protection against leakage.

- **Layer 2** – The 2nd layer of Reign has an ultra-soft cotton top layer, extremely comfortable and soft to the skin.

- **Layer 3** – The 3rd layer of Reign is an Innovative design that offers a Nobel Prize Winning material "Graphene" infused strip. The infused Graphene strip may provide various health benefits to potentially help with circulatory health, cell activity, and metabolic health. In addition, it may help inhibit harmful bacteria growth.

- **Layer 4** – The 4th layer of Reign offers an Air-laid design for extra protection against undesired leakage. Our innovative design is adept at moving the moisture away from the body, so you feel comfortable and dry.

- **Layer 5** – The 5th layer of Reign is designed with a safe, super absorbent polymer, absorbing up to 10x more menstrual flow than traditional sanitary napkins.

- **Layer 6** – The 6th layer of Reign offers reinforcement against moisture. We have added an additional layer of Air-laid. Reign Sanitary Napkins Innovative design is adept at moving the moisture away from the body, not only do you feel comfortable and dry we have gone a step further to add extra protection against leakage.

- **Layer 7** – The 7th layer of Reign offers extreme breathability, which eliminates heat and undesirable moisture. The micro-perforated bottom layer offers air dispersion to keep the area cool and most of all dry. This may help prevent the growth of harmful bacteria and odor.

- **Layer 8** – The 8th layer of Reign offers a durable, agricultural-grade adhesive, without the use of toxic chemicals. Many manufacturers use a construction-grade adhesive, which can be extremely detrimental to a female's most precious area, as well as the planet.

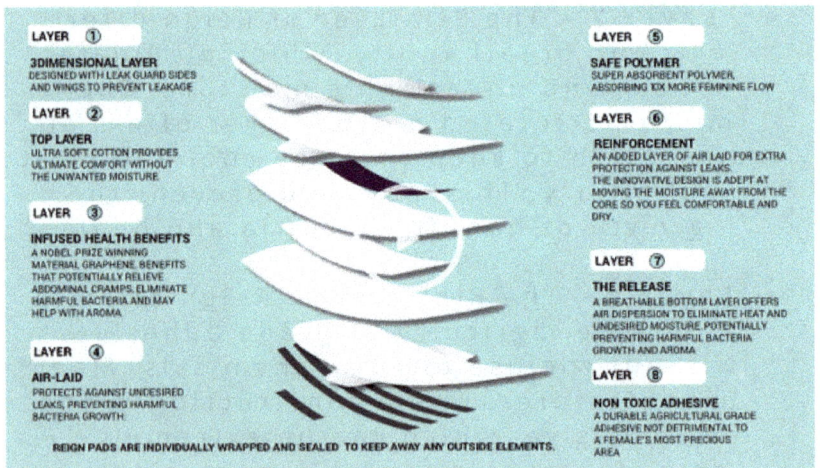

Customer Testimonials

Jewel is passionate about redefining your life with our revolutionary life-changing products.

"As a mother, I love knowing that toxins will not be deposited into my daughters' precious bodies. I feel that if more parents became aware of the health implications that most brands expose their daughters t, Id would see why jewel is the right choice for them also."

Sabrina Ben Salmi
London, UK

"I believe that it's so crucial for young girls and women to have access to products that can keep them safe and comfortable during their cycles; they need and deserve to know that they can trust the products that they use during such a sacred time, and this is what jewel provides, support, protection and comfort."

Lashai Ben Salmi
London, UK

"I advise all women in the world to use toxic-free pads, as it doesn't harm your body; love yourself no matter what."

Yasmine Ben Salmi
London, UK

"I loved the Jewel pads! They stay dry for a long time, they're comfortable, and they don't move around! I wore them during a 14-hour drive to Florida and they kept me comfortable and dry. I did not notice any cramps. Thank you!"

Mary
Ohio

"I just placed my first order and I am currently using them, and these are the best pads I have ever used. I was growing increasingly dissatisfied with other brands and also tried a few organic pads but there was always issues with fit, absorbency or leakage. These pads are so comfortable, fit so well... I love that they are wider with wings, they stay put, I could go on and on. I am so happy and grateful kept searching. I am always concerned with finding a long enough pad for overnight but yours were long!

One Happy Mom

"My 12-year-old just finished today with her cycle. No pain, no cramps and no blood clots; I could not believe it! She experienced having her cycle a month before she turned 11'. I've always had to give her medicine for her cycle. I am one Happy Mom. She normally would wear teen pads. I ordered her the pink pack of Jewel and I ordered the black pack of overnight, but I have not had a chance to use yet.

One Happy Mom

"Jewel is amazing. My husband bought some from a local distributor for me to try out. I wish I had these for the last 3 1/2 decades. Jewel is so comfortable I sometimes forget I am wearing one. My flow is very heavy and usually, I am running to the bathroom every hour with the usual brands at retail stores. I have never felt so comfortable and relaxed during my menstrual flow my entire adult life. I will definitely tell family members and my girlfriends about Jewel. I am thinking about buying packs and giving them as gifts."

Lori
Ohio

"Just gave birth to this beautiful baby about a week ago and was blessed by my Aunt with these amazing Jewel Sanitary Napkins. I can honestly say that they have captured all the waste that's been built up in my body without mess or odor. I have NO CRAMPS at all and it doesn't feel like I have anything on oppose to those hospital pads and other brand that us ladies always wear. Another thing that's brilliant about these pads is it's made for US by US. Who better to create such a product than women? Thanks Auntie love you to the moon and back."

Alisha
New York

"I'm very pleased with Jewel pads. There's no smell at all, even after a full day of wearing one. There are super comfortable. I tried the super heavy flow variety, and even being as large as they are, they were still comfortable. I'd definitely recommend the super heavy for anyone that has a problem with leaking. They cover a large area of a panty and are thin enough for day wear. In short, these are a great product! Thanks so much!"

Tonisha
Florida

"In the middle of June, I wore the Jewel panty liners before my cycle came on. My cycle came on July 12th and it lasted until July 15th for that month!!! Normally, my cycle last about 10 days! These pads are very comfortable and absorb very nicely!! It also reduced my cramps!!"

Lakeisha
Georgia

"I have been using this Jewel Panty Liners since I got them in June. I have had hot flashes since my early twenties. I have subsided the hot flashes tremendously. They are the right size & very comfortable! I am a committed customer!"

Glinda
Texas

"This is my second month using the Jewel Pads and my cycle went from 7 days to 3.5 days. I'm so excited and thankful that you introduced me to such an amazing product. Oh, and my flow was next to nothing. I need the world to know and understand the importance of having a product that can and will change for your life."

Felicia
New Jersey

"I've been using Jewel and I love it! It does not even feel like I'm wearing anything, I can't even believe it and what's even more amazing is that I normally get really bad cramps on day one and no pain at all! Thank you for introducing me to Jewel!"

Heidi
Pennsylvania

"So, what can I say about these pad? One word: FANTASTIC! Not only are they actually comfortable to wear, they're AFFORDABLE! I was cautious of this at first because I have a heavy flow, but all of my doubts went away. I'm so happy I made this choice to try something new. (Also, this doesn't affect your pH balance so that's definitely a plus!)."

Candace
Maryland

"Let me tell you these are so great I always have really strong cramps & they went away I love these pads I'm buying some this week."

Anais
New York

"My name is Gloria. I use the Jewel Premium Sanitary Pads Very Light Panty Liners on a daily basis. They are comfortable to the point I don't realize I have one on. I am secure, comfortable and free from odor. I also get all 4 varieties for my granddaughter. She is elated to have no leakage, no odor, no cramps, no moodiness or bloating when she is on her cycle. She can be active in sports again. I am so glad that we have our Jewel Premium Sanitary Pads for the young all the way to the Seasoned ladies."

Gloria
Louisiana

A friend gave me a sample of the pink pack of moderate flow, she only sampled me two of the pads. I was so satisfied with how comfortable and thin the pad felt I called her for information to order for myself. I definitely noticed the difference, I felt dry for a change and not irritated from my cycle and the store brand pad. I am so comfortable in going out when my cycle is down rather than staying inside during that time of the month. I feel I can enjoy life every day instead of carving out seven days of my life to know I cannot just enjoy normal activity.

Happy Customer

"Even though I heard that most of the products on the market cause us to bleed more because of all the chemicals in it...I'm still in shock that using the ones you gave me made me bleed less and completely shortened my period. I just got it Friday night and I already am done which is crazy. I've been having TERRIBLE periods for 10 years! On top of the endometriosis for the past couple years... this knowledge and these products is literally exactly what I always needed."

Katie
Maryland

I am no longer on my cycle due to a partial hysterectomy. I am still a WOMAN in need of a liner. I am in love with the Very Light Liners, I wear them every day. I exercise three days a week, whether cycling, walking or even outside in the garden, the liners help with any leakage or sweat to keep me dry. Thank you for creating such a super thin liner.

Happy Customer

"The Jewel Pads are amazing, and the graphene is just an added bonus. For 25 years I have been suffering in silence. I tried about everything to ease the extreme cramps, fatigue, headaches, irritation, 7 day long heavy cycles, and emotional stress without any lasting benefits. Then, I tried the Jewel Graphene Sanitary Napkin. It literally changed my life. I have NO cramps now, No Fatigue, Balanced Emotions, and now my cycle is not heavy and only last 3 days now. My life doesn't have to stop just because my cycle is on like before. I stay cool, dry, and fresh. Plus, the pad is super thin! The pad is so comfortable that I forget that I have it on. Plus, it stays in place. I have a peace of mind knowing that I am doing the best thing to support my well-being with the benefits of these pads with the graphene. Plus, I can safeguard my daughter with these pads as well. These are the best pads out there. Thank you for creating these pads and making them accessible to everyone."

Tina
South Carolina

I am no longer on my cycle due to a partial hysterectomy. I am still a WOMAN in need of a liner. I am in love with the Very Light Liners, I wear them every day. I exercise three days a week, whether cycling, walking or even outside in the garden, the liners help with any leakage or sweat to keep me dry. Thank you for creating such a super thin liner.

Happy Customer

TRACK YOUR PERIOD

TRACK YOUR PERIOD

When your doctor asks you for the first day of your last period, are you someone who can tick the date off without thinking, or are you like most girls and women who stare blankly at the doctor's calendar, guessing the date? If you're in the second group, you aren't tracking your menstrual cycles regularly. But keeping a menstrual calendar can be helpful for most girls and women.

Keeping a Record of Your Periods

Tracking your menstrual cycle simply means keeping a record of when you're menstruating, and other information related to your cycle. The best way to get started is to begin with a regular planner or calendar, I usually use an app to track mine, but you can purchase or download anything that helps keep track of your flow.

Your gynaecologist can help you determine the length of your menstrual cycle so that you can keep a menstrual calendar. For most women and girls, period length usually occurs every 21 to 35 days and last 2 to 7 days. Long cycles are considered common for the first few years after your cycle starts.

The months of the year go across the top of this table, and the days go down the side. Towards the end of the day is a space allocated to indicate the number of days your period lasted and your cycle, which shows the number of days between periods.

	J	F	M	A	M	J	J	A	S	O	N	D
1												
2												
3												
4												
5												
6												
7												
8												
9												
10												
11												
12												
13												
14												
15												
16												
17												
18												
19												
20												
21												
22												
23												
24												
25												
26												
27												
28												
29												
30												
31												

PERIOD KEY

NOTES

CYCLE LENGTH

JAN		JUL	
FEB		AUG	
MAR		SEP	
APR		OCT	
MAY		NOV	
JUNE		DEC	

"You are incredible; yes, you are."

- You are incredible; yes, you are. List 3-5 things that are incredible about you.
- Write a letter to a loved one and explain everything you appreciate about them.
- Make a list of 10 acts of kindness that you can do today

_____
_____
_____
_____
_____
_____
_____
_____
_____
_____
_____
_____
_____

MY FIRST DAY

NOTES
MY FIRST DAY

_____
_____
_____
_____
_____
_____
_____
_____
_____
_____
_____
_____ MY FIRST DAY

SURPRISE BONUS CHAPTER: Q & A

SURPRISE BONUS CHAPTER: Q & A

What does a period feel like?

The actual flow of your period doesn't feel like much when it's happening. The chances are, you won't even feel it coming out. When you start your period, you may feel some dampness in your private area — this may be caused by a few spots of blood on your pad or what you are using to hold the blood.

Does having your period smell?

It shouldn't have a specific smell. Menstrual odour happens when menstrual fluid comes in contact with air. When menstrual fluid is absorbed within the vagina, like through a tampon, it is not exposed to the air, so there shouldn't be an odour. If you're worried, change your pads and tampons frequently to help keep the scent away.

Does having your period hurt?

Menstruation doesn't hurt, but some girls and women get cramps or other symptoms during excruciating periods. This is typically due to the hormones your body releases during menstruation that cause the uterus to contract so that it can shed its lining.

I got my period, and I haven't told my mom yet.

Lots of girls have the same concern. If you are a teenager, it is a bit difficult to discuss your period with others, but my advice would be to tell your mother, or an aunt or a close female relative or friend who has been through the same thing because you may learn some things that you may not have known before.

Is it OK to bathe or shower when I have my period?

Yep! Although we may be on your period,, we must maintain healthy hygiene habits, especially as we release blood from our bodies, so it is okay to bathe or shower.

Is there anything I won't be able to do when I have my period?

Your period doesn't have to stop you from doing things you love to do. You can still go to school, help at home, see your friends, play sports and do everything you would typically do. Just remember to have something down there to catch the blood.

How much blood do I lose during my period?

Most girls lose about 1/4 cup of menstrual fluid during their periods (mainly in the first few days). Not to worry, though — your body makes up for it.

"Set yourself FREE."

- Set yourself FREE. List 3-5 ways that you can learn to set yourself free from negative thoughts, behaviours and anything else that is holding me back.
- Make a list of 10 of the funniest memories that still make you laugh every time you think of them.
- Make a list of 10 of the most precious memories that still make you smile every time you think of them.

MY FIRST DAY

NOTES
MY FIRST DAY

--- MY FIRST DAY

BONUS CHAPTER
HER-RAH 1ST BRA

HER-RAH 1ST BRA

Those Budding Breasts, a Mom's Perspective

I was SO scared that something was wrong with me! I remember the very day when I found out my breasts were growing. It was summer, and we were living at our camp on a lake in Maine. I went to my sister, Kathy, and said, "I think I have something wrong here! I feel this kind of small lump, inside my boob, right here!" She started laughing (I didn't think it was funny) and said "Oh, your breasts are starting to grow. Go tell Mom." I went to my mom and told her, and said, "Is this true? What's happening?" She confirmed it, and this was the very beginning of my puberty process. I guess this is how things start for all girls who are entering into their development journey. I was 11 at the time. My mom ended up giving me a hand-me-down bra from my sister. Which, given that I didn't have any experience with getting a first bra, seemed normal to me.

Fast forward a couple of years, and all other kinds of crazy things started happening! My skin was changing, and I needed to wash my face more frequently and with a different kind of soap (getting some breakouts and pimples that had never happened before), I started to wear an antiperspirant, and my emotions were on a roller coaster! Everything I learned, my two older sisters told me or helped me with. My Mom really didn't share a lot, so I felt like I was in the dark on a lot of information. In 6th grade, I came home with an informational pamphlet on "growing up", and an upcoming video in school about the development process. I gave it to my Mom to sign off on and approve, and she cried, asking me if I wanted to attend this. I responded "Yeah, I guess so. I should know about this stuff, right?" It was really awkward having a discussion with my Mom about these sensitive topics, throughout my childhood.

We never communicated on anything that was considered delicate. From an early age, I promised myself that if I ever had a daughter, I would be THE ONE to talk with her about everything and anything, well before she needed to know about it. Fast forward again by 40 years, and I now have a 10-year-old daughter of my own. She is in the 5th grade, and I decided that it was time to have "that talk" with her about development and upcoming body changes. I wanted to be her source of important information.

I didn't want her hearing about breast development, periods, hormones and sex from her peers at school. (I know first-hand that this comes with A LOT of misinformation, and being a nurse, I wanted her to have accurate information). One Sunday in April, I let her know that we were going to lunch together. We were living in Michigan and went to a local pub restaurant that we liked. We sat and ordered our lunch, and I let her know that we were going to talk about "The birds and the bees". She asked "Oh, are the birds, girls, and the bees are boys?" (Very intuitive)! I said "Yes, let's go with that!".

I then started to tell her about upcoming changes to her body, with the first one being breast budding and growth. I also spoke about skin changes, pimples and the importance of keeping her skin clean, sweating and the need for anti-perspirant, hormone changes and the roller coaster of emotions that she might feel, etc… She asked some questions, and I answered them. At the end of our lunch, I gave her a gift bag of a few books on growing up and the development process and told her that these were additional resources for her to look through, but that they did not replace our conversations. I said "if you have any questions, you come to Mommy.

Your friends may tell you a lot of different things, and that's ok. Just make sure that you 'fact check' with me on what's accurate." She promised that she would.

A week later, we were on her Spring Break, and staying with her Godfather and Aunt. She called me into the bedroom one morning to tell me that her breasts were starting to grow, and she needed a bra. I looked at her and said "Well, I think that might be a little early. You're fine." She insisted that she 'needed support' and asked me to check. I did and agreed that we should go bra shopping. McKenna was SO excited! We ended up going to Target, because we could think of anyplace else to go for a bra for young girls. The experience was uber disappointing and anticlimactic. The selections were boring and blah, and a boy waited on her both in the dressing room and at check out! ☹ She said "Mommy, this is so humiliating! And I didn't even find anything cute, as I had hoped!"

McKenna is now 15 years young. For the past 5 years, she has shared every incremental milestone in her development journey (I'm talking about each new pubic hair arrival, going from an A cup to B, then to C, and surpassing her Mom to a D). **where did this come from? She has grown into a beautiful young woman, with her own strong opinions, kind and thoughtful heart, sweet friends, and a solid business mind.

It's a special adventure to share your daughter's journey, don't miss a moment!

Carole Hamm
McKenna's Mom

"Celebrate every new milestone that your body goes through with confidence."

- Celebrate every new milestone that your body goes through with confidence. List 3-5 ways that you can celebrate miles stones in your life.
- Write a **DEAR MONEY** letter and read it out aloud to see whom it reminds you of.
- Write a gratitude letter to yourself and list all the things that you are grateful to yourself for.

_____
_____
_____
_____
_____
_____
_____
_____
_____
_____
_____
_____
_____
_____
_____ MY FIRST DAY

NOTES
MY FIRST DAY

——————————— MY FIRST DAY

MY FIRST DAY
JOURNAL

USE THE FOLLOWING PAGES TO
JOURNAL DAILY

MY FIRST DAY JOURNAL

Writing things down is an effective way of remembering and reflecting on all the fantastic things that happen every day.

No matter how much you write or how little you register, take the time to think about your day; at the end of your journal, you can then go back and treasure those memories.

MY FIRST DAY
JOURNAL

Date: __/__/____
Today I am Grateful For...
_____
_____
_____
_____

What Would Make Today A Great Day?
_____
_____
_____
_____

During the evening just before going to bed take a moment to reflect on your day then List the 3 best things that happened...
_____
_____
_____
_____
_____ MY FIRST DAY

MY FIRST DAY
JOURNAL

Date: __/__/____
Today I am Grateful For...
_____
_____
_____
_____

What Would Make Today A Great Day?
_____
_____
_____
_____

During the evening just before going to bed take a moment to reflect on your day then List the 3 best things that happened...
_____
_____
_____
_____ MY FIRST DAY

MY FIRST DAY
JOURNAL

Date: __/__/____
Today I am Grateful For...
_____
_____
_____
_____

What Would Make Today A Great Day?
_____
_____
_____
_____

During the evening just before going to bed take a moment to reflect on your day then List the 3 best things that happened...
_____
_____
_____
_____

_____ MY FIRST DAY

MY FIRST DAY
JOURNAL

Date: __/__/____
Today I am Grateful For...
_____
_____
_____
_____

What Would Make Today A Great Day?
_____
_____
_____
_____

During the evening just before going to bed take a moment to reflect on your day then List the 3 best things that happened...
_____
_____
_____
_____

MY FIRST DAY
JOURNAL

Date: __/__/____
Today I am Grateful For...
_____
_____
_____
_____

What Would Make Today A Great Day?
_____
_____
_____
_____

During the evening just before going to bed take a moment to reflect on your day then List the 3 best things that happened...
_____
_____
_____
_____

_____ MY FIRST DAY

MY FIRST DAY
JOURNAL

Date: __/__/____
Today I am Grateful For…
_____
_____
_____
_____

What Would Make Today A Great Day?
_____
_____
_____
_____

During the evening just before going to bed take a moment to reflect on your day then List the 3 best things that happened…
_____
_____
_____
_____

——————————— MY FIRST DAY

MY FIRST DAY
JOURNAL

Date: __/__/____
Today I am Grateful For...

_____
_____
_____
_____

What Would Make Today A Great Day?

_____
_____
_____
_____

During the evening just before going to bed take a moment to reflect on your day then List the 3 best things that happened...

_____
_____
_____
_____

MY FIRST DAY

MY FIRST DAY
JOURNAL

Date: __/__/____
Today I am Grateful For…
_____
_____
_____
_____

What Would Make Today A Great Day?
_____
_____
_____
_____

During the evening just before going to bed take a moment to reflect on your day then List the 3 best things that happened…
_____
_____
_____
_____
_____ MY FIRST DAY

MY FIRST DAY
JOURNAL

Date: __/__/____
Today I am Grateful For…
_____
_____
_____
_____

What Would Make Today A Great Day?
_____
_____
_____
_____

During the evening just before going to bed take a moment to reflect on your day then List the 3 best things that happened…
_____
_____
_____
_____

_____ MY FIRST DAY

MY FIRST DAY
JOURNAL

Date: __/__/____
Today I am Grateful For…
_____
_____
_____
_____

What Would Make Today A Great Day?
_____
_____
_____
_____

During the evening just before going to bed take a moment to reflect on your day then List the 3 best things that happened…
_____
_____
_____
_____

_____ MY FIRST DAY

MY FIRST DAY
JOURNAL

Date: __/__/____
Today I am Grateful For…
_____
_____
_____
_____

What Would Make Today A Great Day?
_____
_____
_____
_____

During the evening just before going to bed take a moment to reflect on your day then List the 3 best things that happened…
_____
_____
_____
_____
_____ MY FIRST DAY

MY FIRST DAY
JOURNAL

Date: __/__/____
Today I am Grateful For...
_____
_____
_____
_____

What Would Make Today A Great Day?
_____
_____
_____
_____

During the evening just before going to bed take a moment to reflect on your day then List the 3 best things that happened...
_____
_____
_____
_____

———————————— MY FIRST DAY

MY FIRST DAY
JOURNAL

Date: __/__/____
Today I am Grateful For...
_____
_____
_____
_____

What Would Make Today A Great Day?
_____
_____
_____
_____

During the evening just before going to bed take a moment to reflect on your day then List the 3 best things that happened...
_____
_____
_____
_____

──────────────────── MY FIRST DAY

MY FIRST DAY
JOURNAL

Date: __/__/____
Today I am Grateful For…
_____
_____
_____
_____

What Would Make Today A Great Day?
_____
_____
_____
_____

During the evening just before going to bed take a moment to reflect on your day then List the 3 best things that happened…
_____
_____
_____
_____

MY FIRST DAY

MY FIRST DAY
JOURNAL

Date: __/__/____
Today I am Grateful For...
_____
_____
_____
_____

What Would Make Today A Great Day?
_____
_____
_____
_____

During the evening just before going to bed take a moment to reflect on your day then List the 3 best things that happened...
_____
_____
_____
_____

MY FIRST DAY

MY FIRST DAY
JOURNAL

Date: __/__/____
Today I am Grateful For…
_____
_____
_____
_____

What Would Make Today A Great Day?
_____
_____
_____
_____

During the evening just before going to bed take a moment to reflect on your day then List the 3 best things that happened…
_____
_____
_____
_____ MY FIRST DAY

MY FIRST DAY
JOURNAL

Date: __/__/____
Today I am Grateful For...
_____
_____
_____
_____

What Would Make Today A Great Day?
_____
_____
_____
_____

During the evening just before going to bed take a moment to reflect on your day then List the 3 best things that happened...
_____
_____
_____
_____

MY FIRST DAY

MY FIRST DAY
JOURNAL

Date: __/__/____
Today I am Grateful For...
_____
_____
_____
_____

What Would Make Today A Great Day?
_____
_____
_____
_____

During the evening just before going to bed take a moment to reflect on your day then List the 3 best things that happened...
_____
_____
_____
_____

_____ MY FIRST DAY

MY FIRST DAY
JOURNAL

Date: __/__/____
Today I am Grateful For...
_____
_____
_____
_____

What Would Make Today A Great Day?
_____
_____
_____
_____

During the evening just before going to bed take a moment to reflect on your day then List the 3 best things that happened...
_____
_____
_____
_____
_____ MY FIRST DAY

MY FIRST DAY
JOURNAL

Date: __/__/____
Today I am Grateful For...
_____
_____
_____
_____

What Would Make Today A Great Day?
_____
_____
_____
_____

During the evening just before going to bed take a moment to reflect on your day then List the 3 best things that happened...
_____
_____
_____
_____ MY FIRST DAY

MY FIRST DAY
JOURNAL

Date: __/__/____
Today I am Grateful For…

_____
_____
_____
_____

What Would Make Today A Great Day?

_____
_____
_____
_____

During the evening just before going to bed take a moment to reflect on your day then List the 3 best things that happened…

_____
_____
_____
_____ MY FIRST DAY

ABOUT THE AUTHOR

ABOUT The AUTHOR

MEET THE MIND
BEHIND THE METHOD
https://linktr.ee/YasmineBenSalmi

AS HEARD ON RADIO & AS SEEN ON TV & IN NEWSPAPERS & MAGAZINES

Purpose: To eradicate low self-esteem by liberating 1 million young people through the teaching of self love

Website: https://linktr.ee/YasmineBenSalmi

Guest speaker at Equinix "Global Happiness Speaker Series":
https://www.linkedin.com/posts/ashalalai_happinessday-amilliondreams-happinessday2021-activity-6777873044401614848-JMk-

Yasmine won the Youth Leadership Role Model award via Every Girl Wins Institute 2022 (alongside her big sister Lashai Ben Salmi)

Yasmine was a panel member at the IKAR Global Institute Webinar: The Sky is the Limit alongside panellist: H.E. Adnan Al Noorani, Prince Michael of Yugoslavia and Scott Omelianuk. Moderated by Rory Moore and keynote speaker Alyssa Carson: https://www.linkedin.com/feed/update/activity:6900024539292450817 and this was also shared via the LinkedIn page of The Private Office of Sheikh Saqer Bin Mohamed Al Qasimi: https://www.linkedin.com/posts/the-private-office-of-sheikh-saqer-bin-mohamed-al-qasimi_event-leaders-webinar-activity-6899379648468180992-xk6a

ABOUT *The* AUTHOR

MEET THE MIND
BEHIND THE METHOD

Yasmine's youngest brother 9-year-old Amire is proud to be the youngest ever honorary STEM Ambassador in history for Brunel University London (B.U.L).

B.U.L has given homeschooled families the opportunity to participate in masterclasses for the first time in history, thanks to Lesley Warren.

BEN SALMI FAMILY MANTRA

"BEN SALMI TEAMWORK MAKES THE DREAMWORK

We believe that there is no such thing as failure, only feedback.

We also believe that the journey of one thousand miles begins with a single step in the right direction.

FAMILY ANTHEM

*If you want to be somebody,
If you want to go somewhere,
You better wake up and PAY ATTENTION*

*I'm ready to be somebody,
I'm ready to go somewhere,
I'm ready to woke up and PAY ATTENTION!*

The question is, ARE YOU?

STAY CONNECTED

HTTPS://LINKTR.EE/YASMINEBENSALMI

in Yasmine Ben Salmi

◉ @authoryasminebensalmi

✉ info@dreamingbigtogether.com

> WE ARE ALL CONNECTED
>
> TRUST YOUR HIGHEST THOUGHT, YOUR CLEAREST WORDS AND YOUR GRANDEST FEELING? YOUR HIGHEST THOUGHT IS ALWAYS THE THOUGHT WHICH MAKES YOUR FEEL GOOD. YOUR CLEAREST WORDS ARE THE WORDS WHICH CONTAIN TRUTH AND HONESTY. YOUR GRANDEST FEELING IS LOVE
>
> THE QUESTION IS WHAT WILL YOU CHOOSE TO DO DIFFERENTLY NOW?

www.ingramcontent.com/pod-product-compliance
Lightning Source LLC
Chambersburg PA
CBHW070700100426
42735CB00039B/2355